# Celebrate the Earth

*Psalm 104: Retold & Illustrated*
*by Dorrie Papademetriou*

ST VLADIMIR'S SEMINARY PRESS
2000

Celebrate the Earth
Psalm 104: Retold & Illustrated by
Dorrie Papademetriou


575 Scarsdale Rd., Crestwood, NY 10707
1-800-204-2665



ISBN 0-88141-204-X

Cover art: Dorrie Papademetriou
Cover design: Amber Houx



*For Tom, George and Roman*
*from sunrise to sunset*
*every step of the way*

The publication of this book was made possible in part due to the generosity of Mr. & Mrs. Mark Hudoff.

Dorrie Papademetriou is a graphic designer and artist. She received a Bachelor of Fine Arts from Bowling Green State University. Her work is inspired by her travels through Greece and Turkey, where she studied the colors, the light, as well as the faith and traditions of the people. She lives with her husband and two young sons in Princeton, NJ.

PRINTED IN HONG KONG

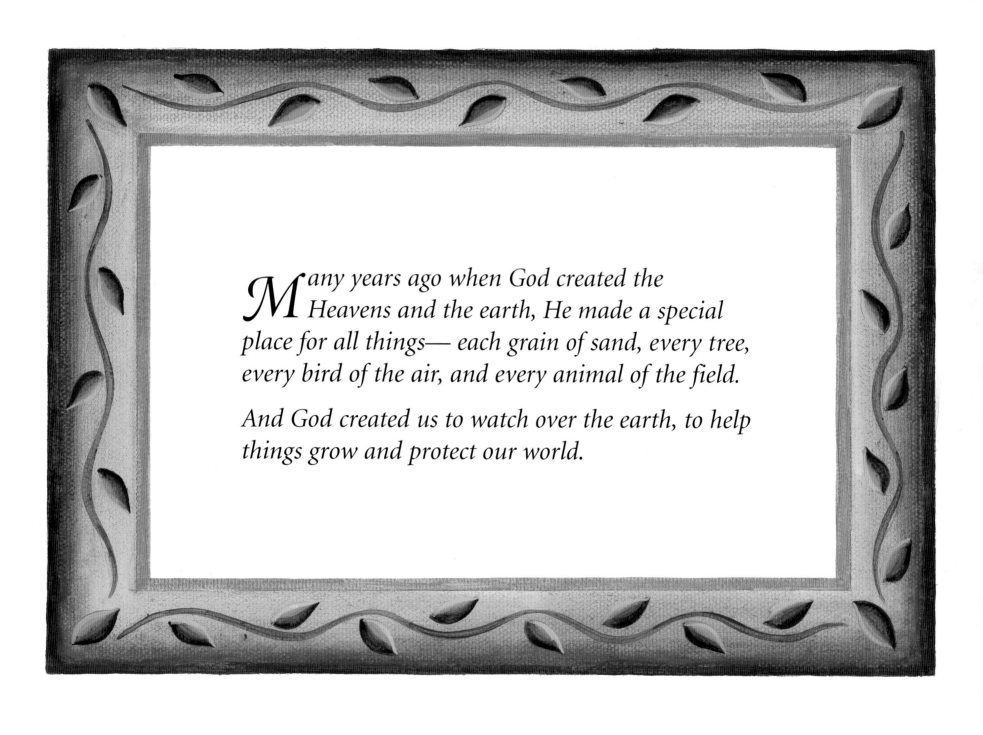

*M*any years ago when God created the Heavens and the earth, He made a special place for all things— each grain of sand, every tree, every bird of the air, and every animal of the field.

And God created us to watch over the earth, to help things grow and protect our world.

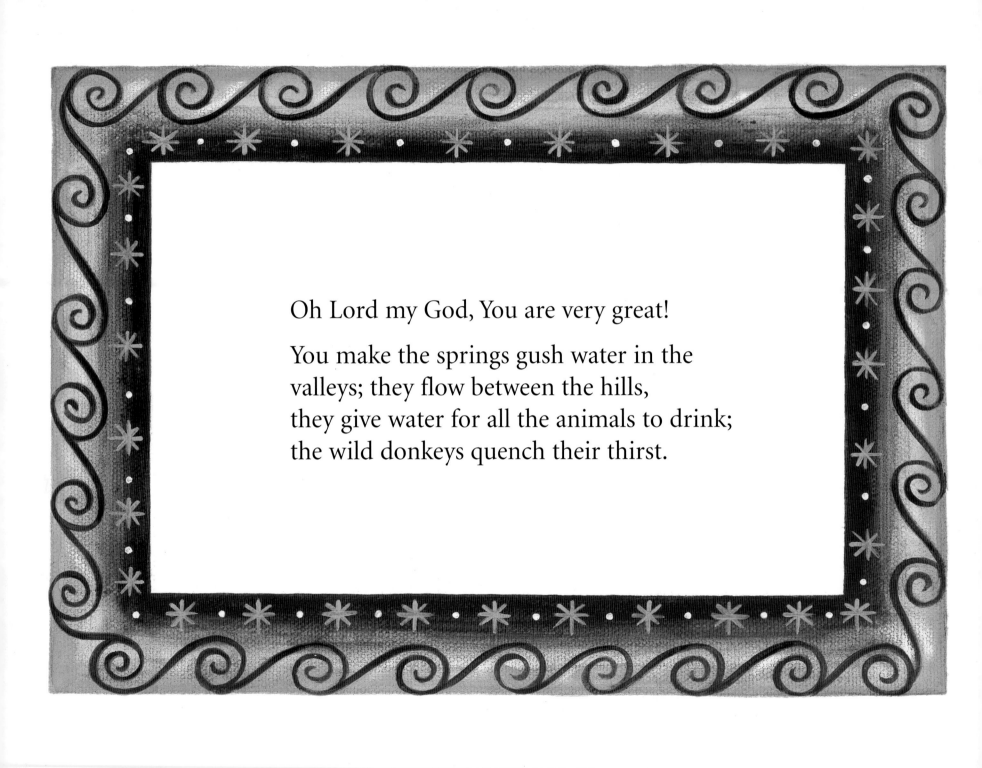

Oh Lord my God, You are very great!

You make the springs gush water in the valleys; they flow between the hills, they give water for all the animals to drink; the wild donkeys quench their thirst.

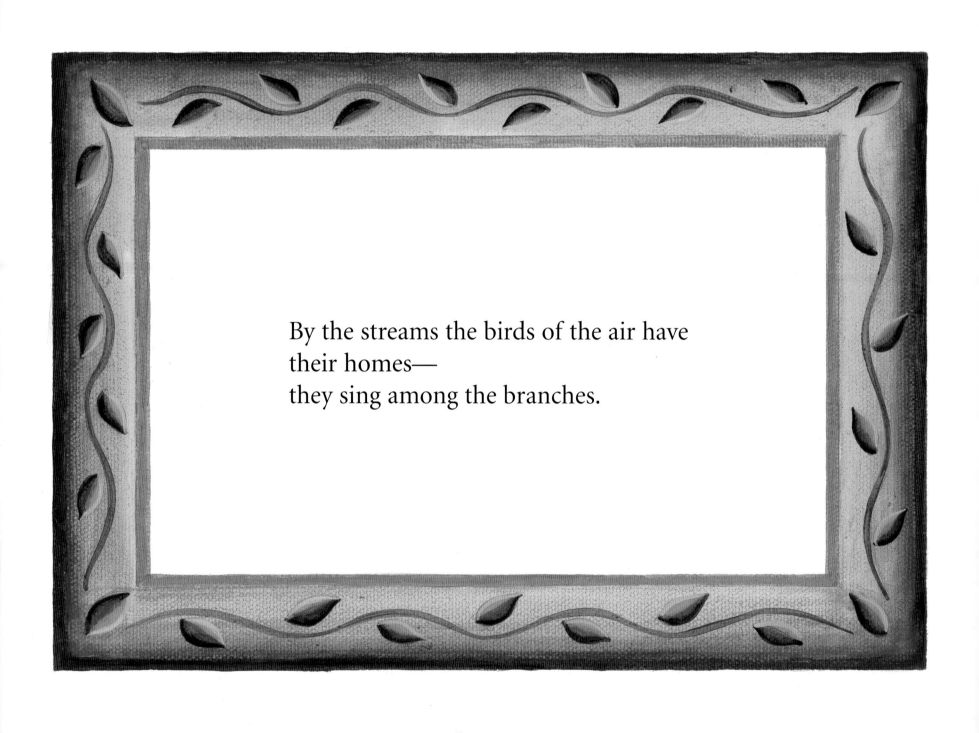

By the streams the birds of the air have
their homes—
they sing among the branches.

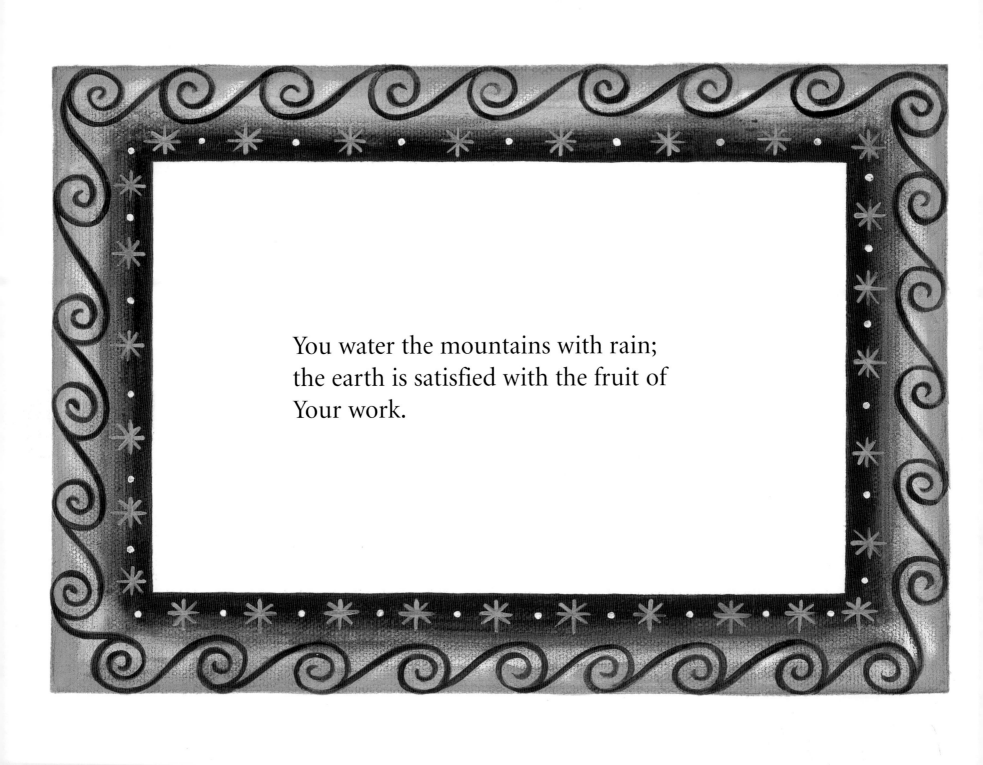

You water the mountains with rain;
the earth is satisfied with the fruit of
Your work.

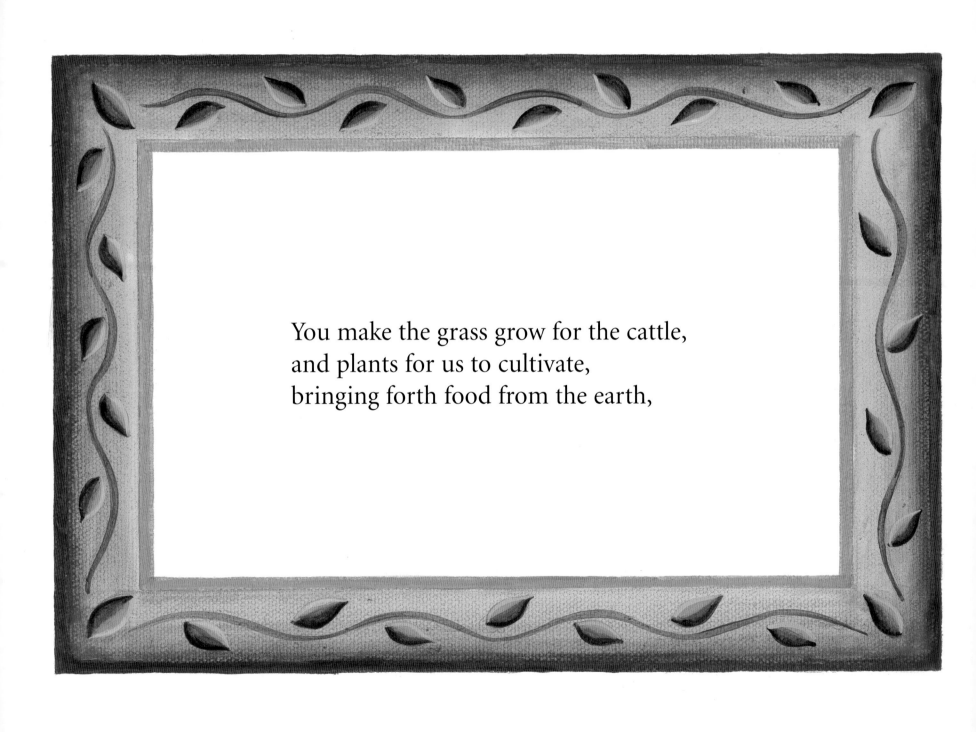

You make the grass grow for the cattle,
and plants for us to cultivate,
bringing forth food from the earth,

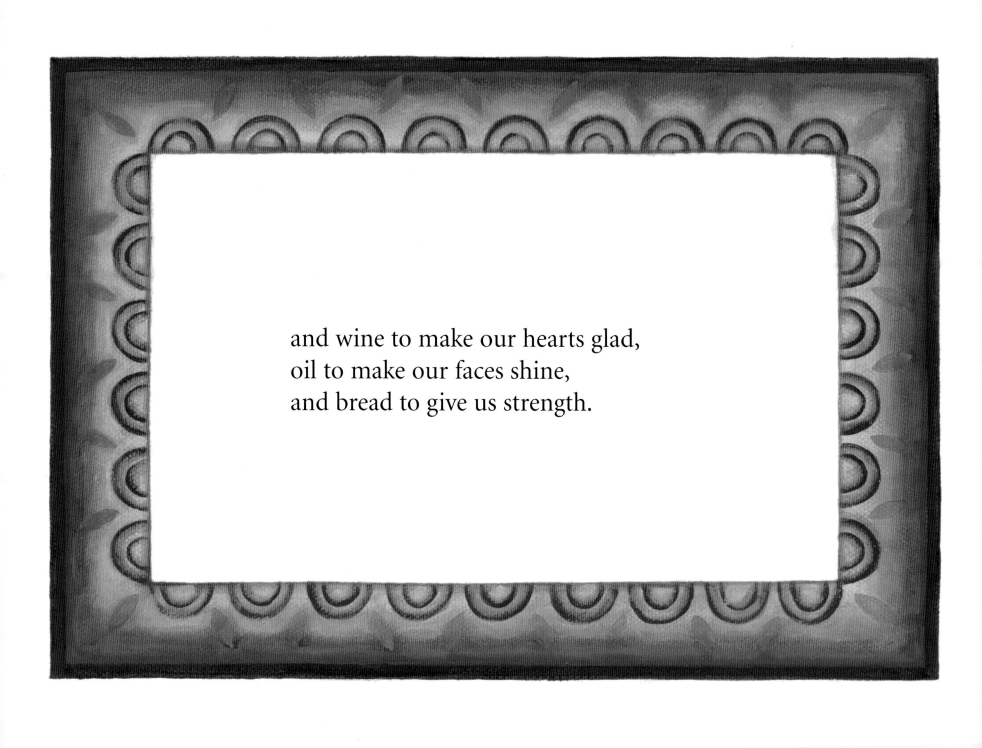

and wine to make our hearts glad,
oil to make our faces shine,
and bread to give us strength.

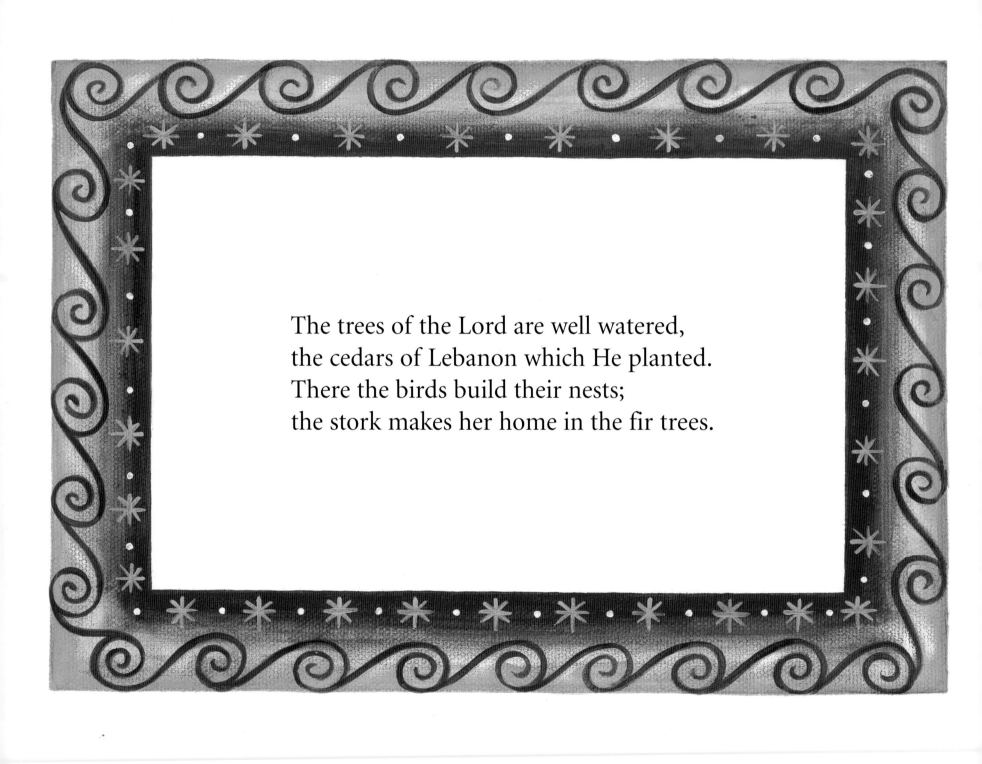

The trees of the Lord are well watered,
the cedars of Lebanon which He planted.
There the birds build their nests;
the stork makes her home in the fir trees.

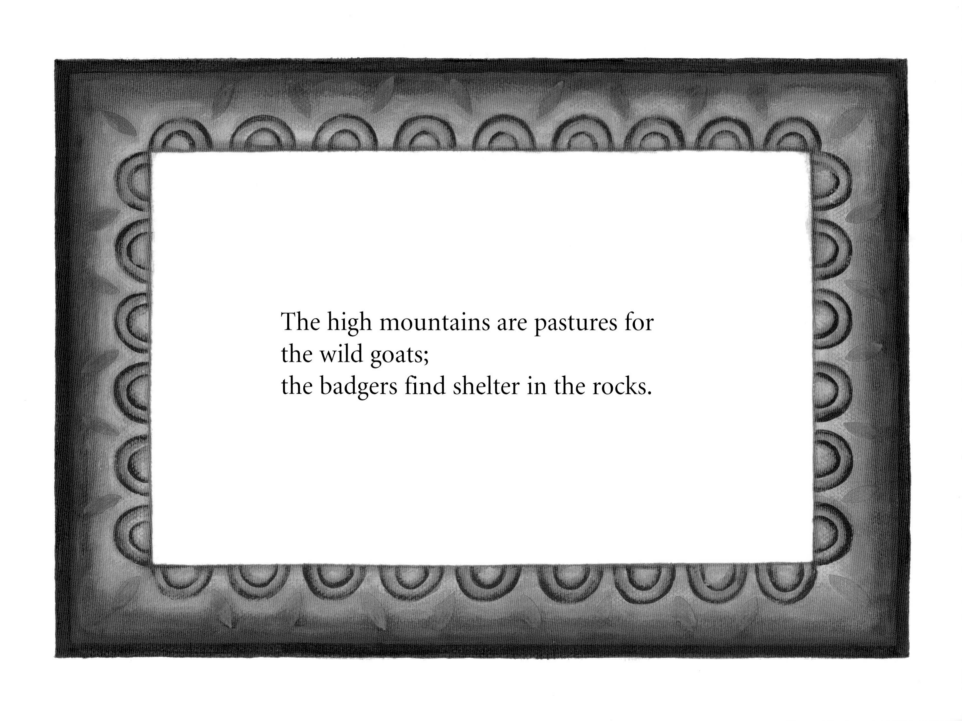

The high mountains are pastures for
the wild goats;
the badgers find shelter in the rocks.

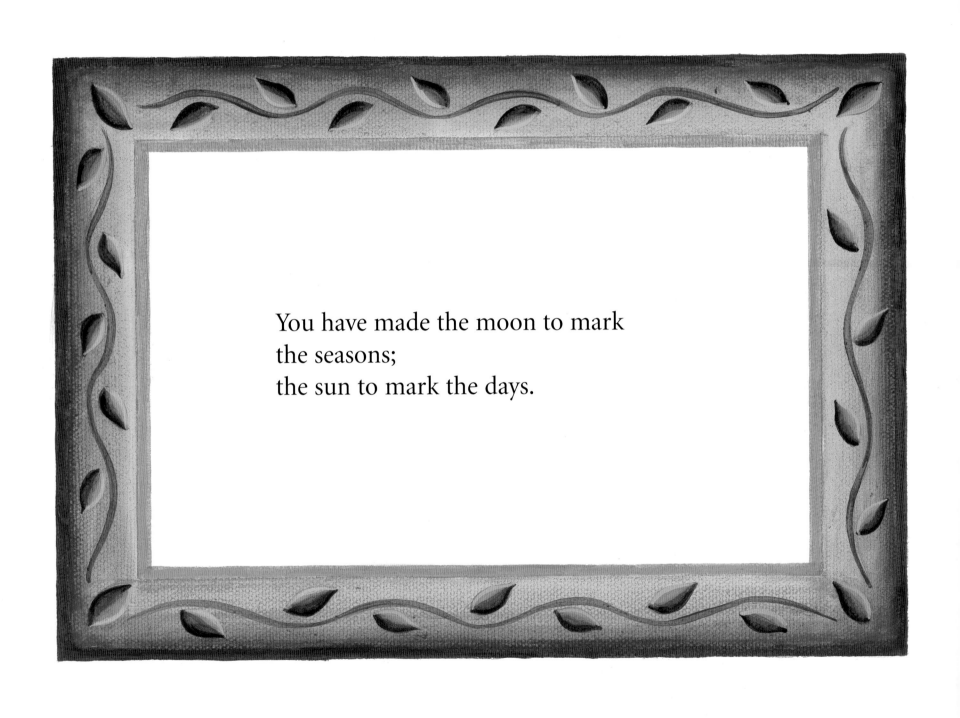

You have made the moon to mark
the seasons;
the sun to mark the days.

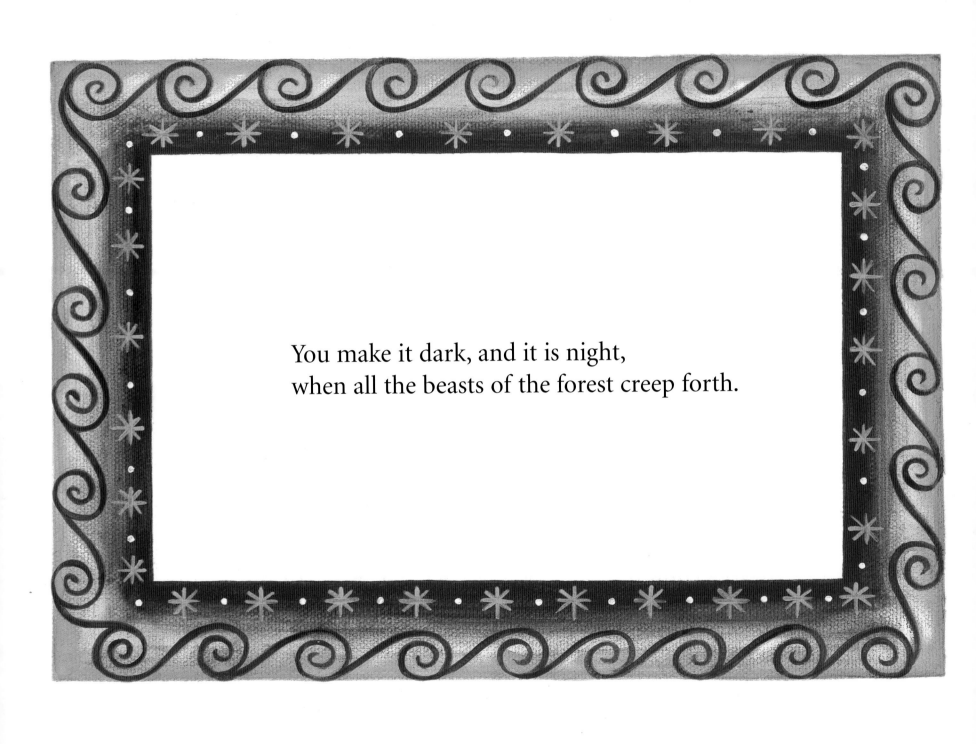

You make it dark, and it is night,
when all the beasts of the forest creep forth.

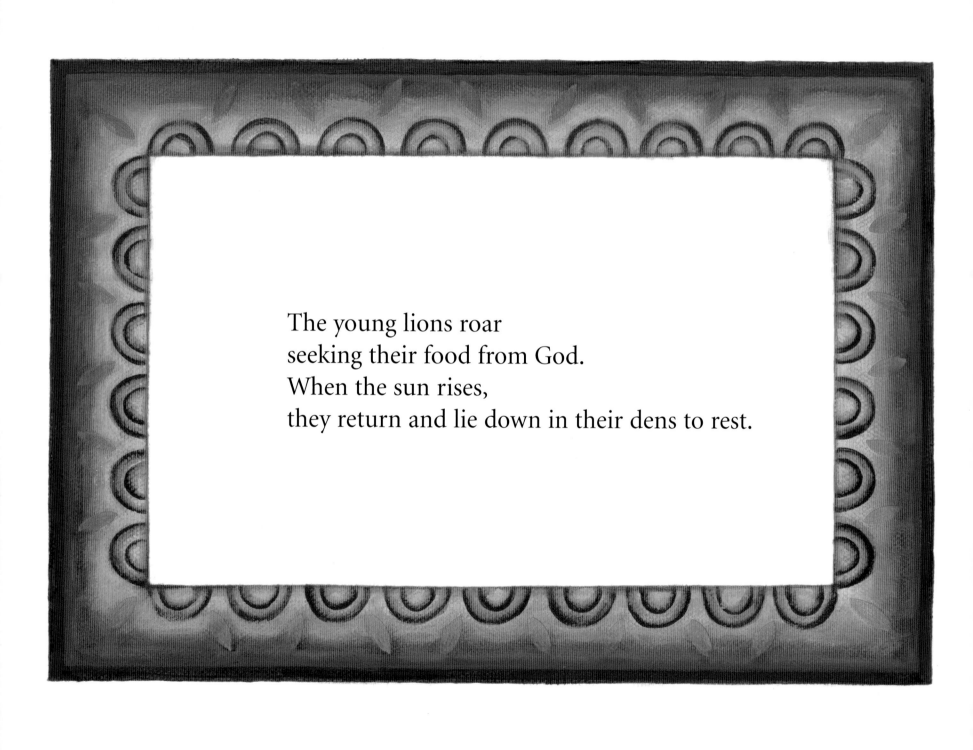

The young lions roar
seeking their food from God.
When the sun rises,
they return and lie down in their dens to rest.

Then we go off to our work until evening.

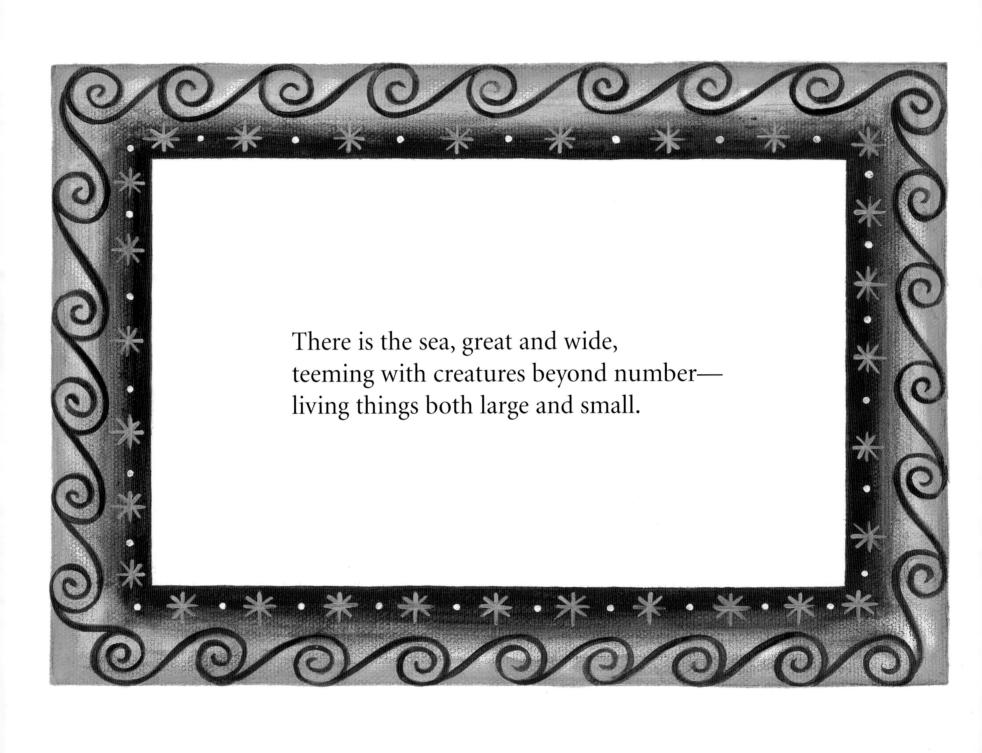

There is the sea, great and wide,
teeming with creatures beyond number—
living things both large and small.

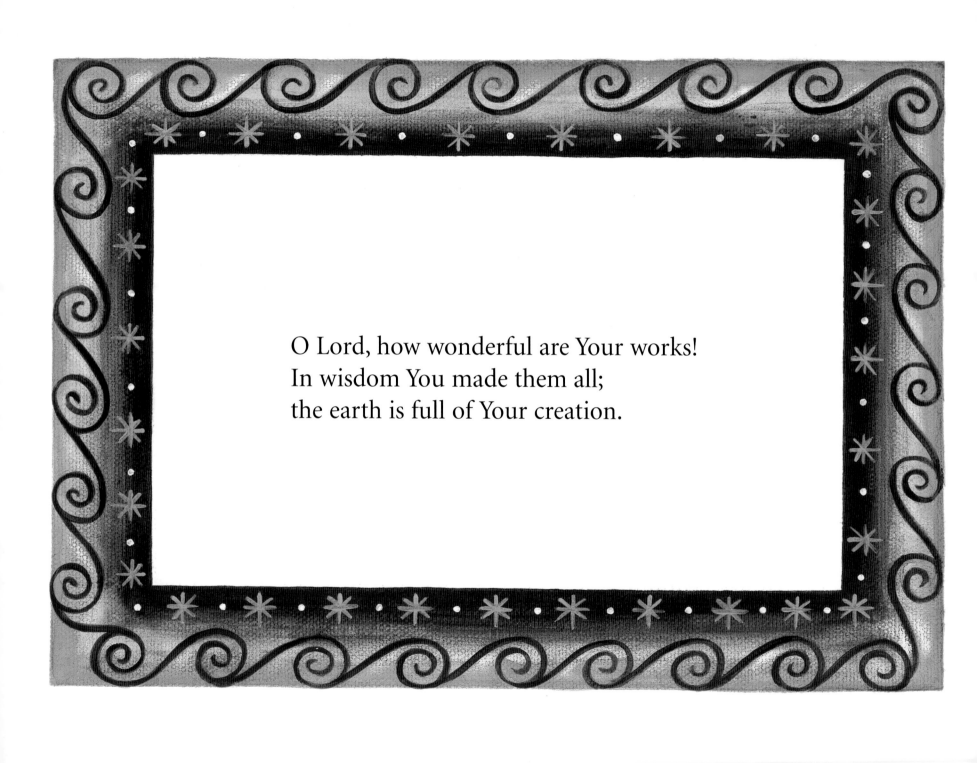

O Lord, how wonderful are Your works!
In wisdom You made them all;
the earth is full of Your creation.

# WISDOM OF THE AGES
## *Words on caring for God's creation*

*Psalm 8*

When I consider your heavens, the work of your fingers, the moon and the stars, which you have set in place, what is man that you are mindful of him, the son of man that you care for him? You made him a little lower than the heavenly beings and crowned him with glory and honor.

*Job 12:7-10*

But ask the animals, and they will teach you, or the birds of the air, and they will tell you; or speak to the earth, and it will teach you, or let the fish of the sea inform you. Which of all these does not know that the hand of the Lord has done this? In His hand is the life of every creature and the breath of all humanity.

*St Basil*
*(329-380 AD)*

O God, enlarge within us the sense of fellowship with all living things, even our brothers, the animals, to whom Thou gavest the earth as their home in common with us.

We remember with shame that in the past we have exercised the high dominion of man with ruthless cruelty so that the voice of the earth, which should have gone up to thee in song, has been a groan of pain. May we realize that they live, not for us alone, but for themselves and for Thee and that they love the sweetness of life.

*St Isaac the Syrian*
*(ca. 7th century AD)*

What is a charitable heart? It is a heart burning with a loving charity for the whole of creation, for men, for the birds, for the beasts, for the demons—for all creatures. He who has such a heart cannot see or call to mind a creature without his eyes being filled with tears by reason of the immense compassion which seizes his heart; a heart which is so softened and can no longer bear to hear of any suffering, even the smallest pain, being inflicted upon any creature. He will pray even for the lizard and reptiles, moved by the infinite pity which reigns in the hearts of those who are becoming united with God.

*St Francis of Assisi*
(1182-1226 AD)

When the brothers were out cutting wood, he would forbid them to cut down the whole tree so that it might grow up again. He ordered the gardeners not to dig up the edges of the gardens so that wild flowers and green grasses could grow and glorify the Father of all things...He picked up worms so they would not be trampled on and had honey and wine set out for the bees in the winter season. He called by the name of brother all animals...

*St Herman of Alaska*
(ca. 1756-1837 AD)

What could be better, higher, more worthy of love and more splendid than Our Lord Jesus Christ himself, who created the firmament, and adorned everything, gave life to everything, who keeps everything, feeds everything and loves everything—who is himself love, more splendid than all

men! Should you not love God above all things, wish for Him and seek Him?

*Fyodor Mikhail Dostoevsky*
(1821-1881 AD)

Love all God's creation, the whole of it and every grain of sand. Love every leaf, every ray of God's light! Love the animals, love the plants, love everything. If you love everything, you will perceive the divine mystery in things.

# Psalm 104:10-25

## A PSALM OF DAVID

You make springs gush forth in the valleys;
 they flow between the hills,
they give drink to every beast of the field;
 the wild asses quench their thirst.
By them the birds of the air have their habitation;
 they sing among the branches.
From Your lofty abode You water the mountains;
 the earth is satisfied with the fruit of Your work.

You cause the grass to grow for the cattle,
 and plants for man to cultivate,
that he may bring forth food from the earth,
 and wine to gladden the heart of man,
oil to make his face shine,
 and bread to strengthen man's heart.
The trees of the Lord are watered abundantly,
 the cedars of Lebanon which he planted.
In them the birds build their nests;
 the stork has her home in the fir trees.

The high mountains are for the wild goats;
 the rocks are a refuge for the badgers.
You made the moon to mark the seasons;
 the sun knows its time for setting.
You make darkness and it is night,
 when all the beasts of the forest creep forth.
The young lions roar for their prey,
 seeking their food from God.
When the sun rises, they get them away
 and lie down in their dens.
Man goes forth to his work
 and to his labor until the evening.

O Lord, how manifold are Your works!
 In wisdom You have made them all;
 the earth is full of Your creatures.
Yonder is the sea, great and wide,
 which teems with things innumerable,
 living things both small and great.

*O Lord my God, You are very great!*